MARIE-JOSÉE THIBAULT

1

THE HOLY POPE
Saint John Paul II
SPEAKS

The Holy Pope Saint John Paul II Speaks - Book 1

Published by Abba Books LLC
abbabooksllc@gmail.com
Copyright © 2023 Marie-Josée Thibault

All Rights Reserved

No part of this publication may be reproduced, distributed, or transmitted in any form or by any means, including photocopying, recording, or other electronic or mechanical methods, without the prior written permission of the publisher.

First Edition, 2023
Designed and Edited by Abba Books LLC
ISBN: 979-8-9887805-4-0

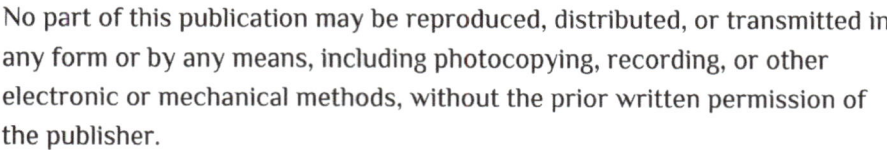

Abba Books LLC
34972 Newark Blvd, #441
Newark, CA 94560

www.abbamyfatheriloveyou.com
https://www.facebook.com/AbbaILoveYouBooks/

Thy Peace on Earth must be achieved. No light, no litany must be spared to honor Thy Grace.
-Saint Paul

CONTENTS

Preface VI	**Chap 10** 25	**Chap 20** 65
Chap 1 1	**Chap 11** 31	**Chap 21** 69
Chap 2 3	**Chap 12** 33	**Chap 22** 71
Chap 3 5	**Chap 13** 37	**Chap 23** 75
Chap 4 7	**Chap 14** 41	**Chap 24** 77
Chap 5 9	**Chap 15** 45	**Chap 25** 79
Chap 6 13	**Chap 16** 51	**Chap 26** 83
Chap 7 17	**Chap 17** 55	**Chap 27** 85
Chap 8 19	**Chap 18** 59	**Chap 28** 87
Chap 9 21	**Chap 19** 63	**Chap 29** 91
		Chap 30 93
		Chap 31 99
		Chap 32 101
		Chap 33 103
		Chap 34 105
		Chap 35 107

PREFACE

I have been regularly blessed with visitations from Saint John Paul II over the past few years. He typically shows up on Friday or Saturday mornings and appears in my living room next to my Marian shrine. We speak, discuss, and pray together, and then he disappears. He is my spiritual director: He follows my progress and instructs me, gives me encouragement when I feel overwhelmed, scolds me when I deserve it, explains things I fail to understand, and—above all—blesses me. Lastly, he ordered me to publish these messages to humanity.

"I say unto you, I say unto you verily: God loves you, and He has assigned your soul to me in order for me to take it to Him as rapidly as possible through the Holy Name of Jesus Christ and the ever-Immaculate Heart of Mary. Your soul is in my hands. At this time, you are reading these lines, and it will be here forever and ever."

Amid the noise of modern times, Saint John Paul II's unwavering and heavenly voice rises like a timeless song, inviting us to a totally different rhythm.

This book offers you the unique opportunity to dwell in the mystical presence of a visionary saint whose words, actions, and spirit are more relevant today than they were while he was alive. As you flip through these pages, be prepared to engage with Saint John Paul II himself—allow the eternal spirit of the saint to guide you on a path of intimate companionship, mystical bonding, and holy transformation.

Make sure not to miss Books 1 and 2.

Saint John Paul II, I love you!

Marie-Josée

THE HOLY POPE SPEAKS: Saint John Paul II

My children of the whole earth, I am in Heaven and I speak to you through the essence of Saint Paul on earth, Marie-Josée T.

Listen to me, listen to me well. I am Saint John Paul II and I have several extraordinary Messages to communicate to you from Heaven. The earth will undergo terrible changes shortly, yet these events are ordained by God the Father Almighty in order to restore an axis of Spirituality based solely on Christ. These Messages given here, sanctioned by God the Father Almighty, are critical to enable you to survive the disasters to come.

I love you and I will help you plan and live through the Great Darkness which will befall the whole earth and which is approaching fast.

Alleluia! Alleluia! Alleluia! Blessed is he who listens to my Words, the Words of Saint John Paul II, for that one shall be saved.

Amen. Alleluia!

THE HOLY POPE SPEAKS: Saint John Paul II

My beloved children of the earth, come into my arms! When I was Pope at the Vatican, my duties and responsibilities were vast and complex and the Lord Jesus Christ and the Blessed Virgin Mary greatly helped me in living a unique and effective Pontificate for Catholics worldwide.

After my death in 2005, and my passage into the Great Beyond, my duties and responsibilities continued. In fact, they have intensified in terms of global significance and luminous effectiveness.

Verily, verily, I say unto you, my global Powers at this moment of history are greater and more influential with regard to the future of humanity than during my life on earth.

Such is the desire of the Most High, the Father Almighty, Who gave me the Grace of Compassion and of Holiness, for ever and ever, and for Whom my gratitude and appreciation are infinite, through the Holy Name of Jesus Christ and the Immaculate Heart of Mary.

Alleluia! Alleluia! Alleluia! Blessed is he who walks in the Light with Christ Jesus, for shortly this one will meet me as well.

Amen. Alleluia!

THE HOLY POPE SPEAKS: Saint John Paul II

My children of the whole earth, I am Saint John Paul II. My Holiness has not been authorized by man, but it has been granted by the Grace and the Benevolence of God the Father, the Creator of all things visible and invisible, our Almighty. Your soul is what matters in your life—nothing else is relevant in the Eyes of God.

During my earthly life, amid the social, political, and religious scene in which I participated, I was in a position to meet thousands and thousands of souls. Among these souls, truly very few of them were elevated and close to God. Unfortunately, the deep and miserable involutionary state of humanity leaves little chance for the soul to ascend to God.

I say unto you, I say unto you verily, take care of your soul, and cherish every moment dedicated to your Creator, through the Holy Name of Jesus Christ and the Immaculate Heart of Mary, in order to prepare your soul for the severe and detailed inspection that is the Judgment of God. For the passage that is death is near in the physical world, where time passes so quickly... I remember!

Alleluia! Alleluia! Alleluia! Blessed is he who prepares his death today, for today, God the Father assesses this soul through the reading of this book blessed by His Almighty Hands.

Amen. Alleluia!

THE HOLY POPE SPEAKS — Saint John Paul II

My beloved children, I am delighted to speak to you today through the essence of Saint Paul on earth, Marie-Josée T. She has written and published other books dictated by other Saints as well as by the Virgin Mary. I am infinitely grateful to Marie-Josée for her dedication to the Plan of Salvation conceived by God the Father, of which she is an instrument of peace on earth, and above all, to God the Father Almighty for so much Mercy offered to you today. For the end times are approaching and this blessed book will guide you through how to protect yourself during this difficult future.

I also invite you to read the other books dictated to Marie-Josée. The Saints in Heaven are alerted to the upcoming events and they wish to help you and contribute to the salvation of your soul. For the Judgment of God will soon befall all creatures that He created on earth...

Alleluia! Alleluia! Alleluia! Blessed is he who reads this book and listens to my Words, for I am Saint John Paul II and my current mission in Heaven surpasses the mission of my Pontificate on earth, and my influence over all of humanity is increasing, through the Grace of Christ our Savior and the Mercy of God.

Amen. Alleluia! †

THE HOLY POPE SPEAKS Saint John Paul II

My friends, my children, I speak to you from Heaven and I love you. My role as Pope for the Catholic world had been decided and executed by God the Father Almighty, Who decides everything, with regard to everything, at all times.

Similarly, God our Father makes all Decisions regarding your life. Therefore, turn to Him at all times, present your whole life to Him as evidence of your understanding of His complete domination over you, by virtue of His Divine and Immutable Will, and surrender yourself completely to His Love.

The Father loves you much more than you can imagine and His Love will be manifested to you in your life in different forms: fantastic graces, opportunities for Spiritual growth, relief of pain and suffering, and above all, the Gift of the Precious Blood of His Only Son, the Lamb Redeemer, the Savior of the world, our Christ Jesus, the Light of the world.

Alleluia! Alleluia! Alleluia! Blessed is he who loves God, and who turns to Him at all times, for God the Father will show him His Love even more and a thousand times over.

Amen. Alleluia!

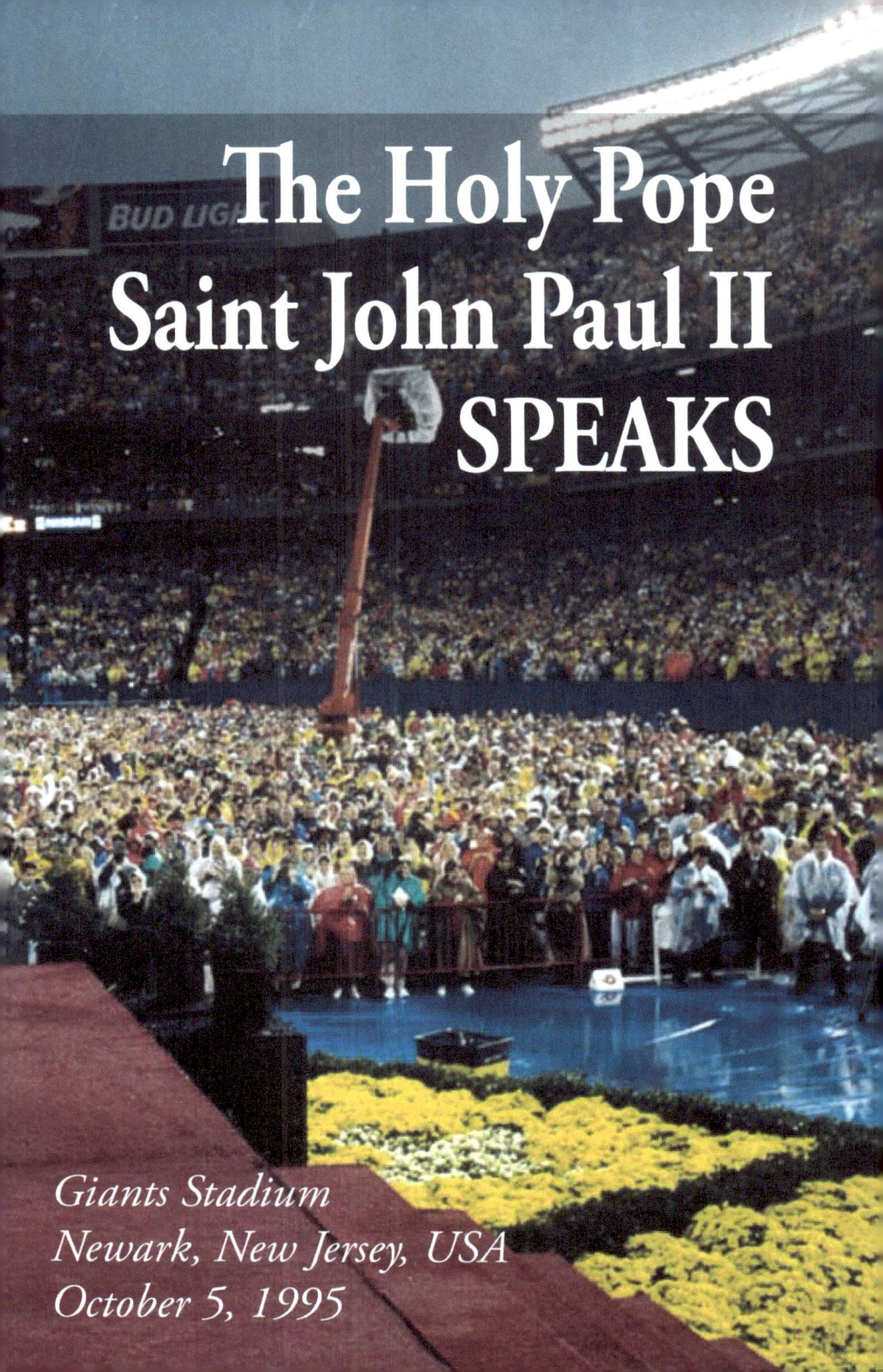

THE HOLY POPE SPEAKS Saint John Paul II

My children, be generous with your time devoted to God. The torments of life, the obstacles of any kind, and especially the impediments to Spiritual growth, are quickly removed when the soul turns directly to God, through Christ Jesus, His Only Son.

Pray! Pray! Pray! As often as you can, pray! Pray during the short moments of the day, going here and there, and turn your heart to Him! Recite the Lord's Prayer when you are going up the stairs or taking the elevator! Say "My God, I love you!" dozens of times per day!

THE HOLY POPE SPEAKS — Saint John Paul II

And soon, very soon, everything will become clear in your life, peace and harmony will fill your heart permanently and enduringly, and opportunities for your growth at all levels will multiply. For God is seeking your attention through the trials and tribulations of life, and wishes only to be your unique Source of comfort and solution, through the imitation of the Virtues and Ways of Christ, His Cosmic Messenger, His Beloved Son.

*Alleluia! Alleluia! Alleluia! Blessed is he
who prays to God directly, for just as directly,
God will overflow him with graces,
through the Holy Name of Jesus
and the Immaculate Heart of Mary.*

Amen. Alleluia!

THE HOLY POPE SPEAKS — Saint John Paul II

My children, listen carefully to my Words, for my Words have been sanctified by God Himself. God the Father loves you, much more than you can imagine, each and every one of you.

Be not afraid of what is approaching upon earth, be not afraid of anything. Faith in God the Father, through Christ Jesus, my Savior, and the Virgin Mary, my Mother, will protect you and will guide you through every obstacle you will come across, for the simple reason that He is at the Source of all obstacles. Who else but the One who sends you a test can best help you pass this same test?

God the Father loves you, God the Father will test you, God the Father will guide you and support you through the tests that are approaching, and God the Father will welcome you when you will exit the tests in triumph.

God alone is all you need, through the Love and the Light of His Divine Creations: Christ His Son, the Virgin Mary, the Holy Spirit, the Saints in Paradise, the Angels of God. We here are all ruled and loved by the Supreme Power of the Loving God, Only God through all ages.

Glory and honor to God the Father Almighty, Who loves us all so much, on earth as in Heaven!

Amen. Alleluia.

THE HOLY POPE SPEAKS — Saint John Paul II

My children, be attentive to your heart. In your heart resides all the information necessary to the elucidation of the problems in your life—all the solutions, all the prayers, all the peace, all the Kingdom of God the Father.

Your heart is the physical seat of the soul and the soul is united to God, no matter where you are or what you do. This is why we can communicate with you, for your soul is always available to our coming in and out, which is unfolding in the heart, as God wishes. For the Creator is always united with His Creation and directs It at all times and in all places.

Alleluia! Alleluia! Alleluia! Blessed is he who awakens to the presence of the Kingdom of God in the heart, the seat of the soul, which belongs to God.

Amen. Alleluia!

THE HOLY POPE SPEAKS — Saint John Paul II

My children, remember me. A Pope at a young age (58 years), I had great zeal and determination in order to accomplish my mission to perfection. I was perfectly aware that this mission was conceived and monitored by God the Father Almighty.

Yes, I had developed a very intimate relationship with God, in the very depth of my human heart. My faith in Him grew day by day, and I have witnessed countless Miracles He performed for me in order, precisely, to strengthen and deepen my faith in Him, through Jesus my Savior and Mary my Sweet Mother.

My human heart was transformed into a Divine Heart after the passage that is death—in 2005. My joy was boundless at being admitted to the Kingdom of Heaven, where I was greeted and embraced by Christ, my Savior and my King; the Virgin Mary, my Divine Mother; the Holy Spirit; the other Saints in Paradise; the pure Souls and the Angels of God.

THE HOLY POPE SPEAKS — Saint John Paul II

All, without exception welcomed me with exhilaration and rejoicing unparalleled in my life. Such relief to be freed of an old and sick body! Such ineffable joy of living in the majestic beatitudes of Paradise! Such Love abides here in Paradise!

Come my children, come join us in Paradise, which is awaiting you after the passage that is death and which will be the crowning of your life on earth! Be not afraid at all of the trials and tribulations of your life, as these obstacles build your stairway leading up to Paradise! This stairway of pain and suffering has been chosen—and carefully and lovingly elaborated—by God the Father in order to ensure your climb all the way here!

Remain in the faith and the firm belief that Paradise truly exists and is awaiting you after the passage that is death. I will welcome you at the Gates of Paradise; I make this promise to you today.

Alleluia! Alleluia! Alleluia! Blessed is he who believes in Paradise, for Paradise is his!

Amen. Alleluia!

J ✝✝✝✝✝✝ PII

THE HOLY POPE SPEAKS Saint John Paul II

My children, rejoice and be glad in your heart, for God the Father has leaned over you and has allowed you to read these Lines and to hear my Words, the Holy Words of Saint John Paul II. My role in your life has been initiated during my life on earth. God the Father, our Creator of all, the Supreme Sovereign toward all, gave me the Grace to continue to watch over the Spiritual and Catholic development of your soul.

My role in Heaven, therefore, is an extension of my role on earth. However, my role here is much broader and more significant with respect to your soul. My role is to ensure that you, dear reader, are admitted here in Paradise, after the passage that is death. In addition, I promise to proceed to the sanctification of your soul, which is possible if you observe all the commands of the Church and those given here in this book, through the Holy Name of Jesus, my Savior, and Mary, my Mother.

THE HOLY POPE SPEAKS — Saint John Paul II

I make you a promise today, dear precious soul, dear child of God Who loves you, to personally welcome you to Paradise on the day of your arrival here, and to celebrate your Holiness according to the graces you will obtain on earth, with Christ, the Lamb of God.

Alleluia! Alleluia! Alleluia!
Blessed is he who reads these Lines and listens to my Words,
for I, Saint John Paul II, shall sanctify him
through the Holy Name of Jesus,
Christ the Savior, the Light of the world.

Amen.

J ☨☨☨☨☨ PII

Thy Peace on Earth

Poland Countryside

THE HOLY POPE SPEAKS — Saint John Paul II

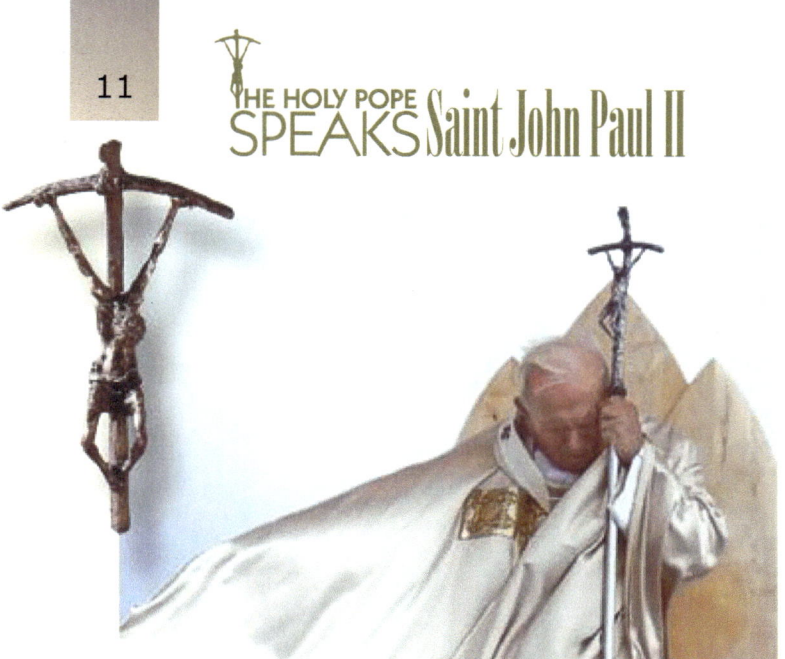

My children, always remain firm in your faith in Christ Jesus. He alone is the Savior of the world, He alone is the Light of the world, He alone is the Lamb Redeemer. Look no further for what is the Source of everything!

*I embrace you and I bless you
in the Name of the Father, and of the Son,
and of the Holy Spirit.*

Amen. So be it.

12 THE HOLY POPE SPEAKS Saint John Paul II

My children to whom I wish happiness on earth, listen to me well. My Words are Sacred for they represent a Message originating directly from the Mouth of God, the Father Almighty.

I say unto you, I say unto you verily, God loves you and He has assigned your soul to me in order to take it to Him as rapidly as possible, through the Holy Name of Jesus Christ and the ever-Immaculate Heart of Mary. Your soul is in my hands, at this time you are reading these Lines, and it will be herein for ever and ever.

Be not afraid! I have said it a thousand times during my life on earth, and I will say it again here and every day for the rest of your life: be not afraid!

God loves you. God expresses His Love in many ways, including this book you are holding in your hands. For this book blessed by God Himself is much more than a collection of papers and written Words; this book is a Sacred Vehicle of Messages from the Great Beyond, prepared and executed under the Orders and the Supreme Authority of our Creator of all, the Solar Father.

THE HOLY POPE SPEAKS: Saint John Paul II

For God loves you and God Himself writes these Lines through me, Saint John Paul II, sanctified by Him, and the essence of Saint Paul on earth. Marie-Josée and I are messengers of God the Father Almighty, as well as of several other Saints in Paradise Who also speak to you through her. For it pleases God the Father to speak to you now, through us, according to His Great Plan of Salvation.

Alleluia! Alleluia! Alleluia! Blessed are the messengers of God on earth as in Heaven, and beware those who decry these messengers of God, for God Himself in this is offended.

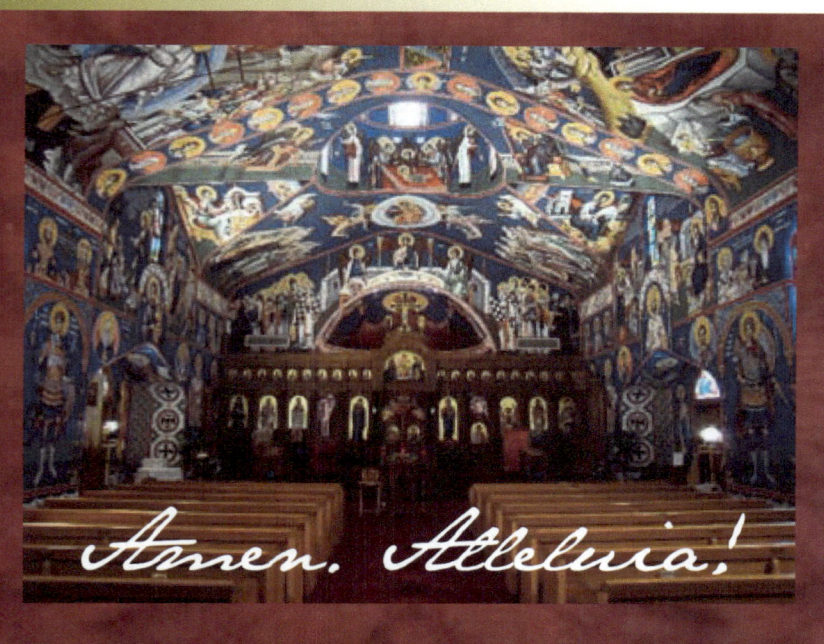

Amen. Alleluia!

J ✝✝✝✝✝✝ PII

THE HOLY POPE SPEAKS — Saint John Paul II

My little children, come into my arms now! I bless you in the Name of the Father, and of the Son, and of the Holy Spirit.

I speak to you from Heaven, and simultaneously, I speak to you within your heart. Do not ignore the moments of inspiration that you will experience shortly, as well as the new states of consciousness centered on Christ and the Mystical and Spiritual experiences that will take place in your life. For the Kingdom of Heaven is settling in comfortably within your heart, at this time you are reading these Lines, and all the Graces and Miracles that you have hoped for all your life will very shortly materialize.

Pray, my children, pray! Ask for the solution to all your problems: ask for the relief of financial hardship, ask for peace and harmony in your household, ask for opportunities to deepen your knowledge of God and of all His messengers, and unto you these shall be given.

Pray, my children, pray again! Pray for the healing of your own body, or the well-being of your loved ones; pray for the emotional healing of your inner suffering, pray for the healing of wounds and trauma of the past and of childhood. For God is very sensitive to your prayers, as of today, by virtue of the redemption that is enclosed within this wonderful book you are holding in your hands, utilizing the Voice and Heart of Saint John Paul II to reach you—my Voice and Heart sanctified by God Himself.

THE HOLY POPE SPEAKS: Saint John Paul II

Let us together demonstrate to God the Father Almighty our infinite gratitude for so much Mercy that is offered to you today by reciting the Lord's Prayer:

Our Father who art in Heaven,
hallowed be thy Name.
Thy Kingdom come.
Thy Will be done on earth as it is in Heaven.
Give us this day our daily bread,
and forgive us our trespasses,
as we forgive those who trespass against us,
and lead us not into temptation,
but deliver us from evil.
For Thine is the Kingdom,
the Power,
and the Glory,
for ever and ever.

Amen.

J ✝ ✝ ✝ ✝ ✝ PII

THE HOLY POPE SPEAKS — Saint John Paul II

My beloved children, listen to me well. Events that lie ahead will be difficult for each and every one of you on earth. I will be among you on earth—I make this promise to you today.

The whole Heaven will assist you according to the extent of your faith and hope in us and in God the Father Almighty. Several levels of instruction and preparation will be given to you in order to make you strong and informed of all the phases that will take place during the tragic moments to come.

Remember that God the Father loves you and will protect you always. The proof of His Love is manifested further here, for at this very moment, I bless you in the Name of the Father, and of the Son, and of the Holy Spirit.

THE HOLY POPE SPEAKS: Saint John Paul II

Saint John Paul II, the Pope you have known and loved, in whom you have put all your trust and all your hope, will never abandon you. I promise you.

I am Saint John Paul II. I love you and I will be with you forever—and beyond—and I will hold you in my arms from the very first moments of your glorious entry into Paradise. I promise you.

I love you. God loves you. I bless you in the Name of the Father, and of the Son, and of the Holy Spirit. Amen.

So be it. Alleluia!

J ✝ ✝ ✝ ✝ ✝ P II

THE HOLY POPE SPEAKS: Saint John Paul II

My children,
I bless you in the Name of the Father, and of the Son, and of the Holy Spirit. Today is a special day in your life, for today, Saint John Paul II, your Friend and your Benefactor, on earth as in Heaven, Saint John Paul II who is speaking to you now and who loves you, personally introduces you to God Almighty, through my Holy intercession.

For God the Father Himself has decided so—the same way He has decided and has executed my obtention of the Grace of Holiness, and for which I owe Him my infinite gratitude, through the merits of Jesus, my Savior, and the Immaculate Heart of Mary, my Mother.

God the Father loves you. I know absolutely every detail of your life—and above all, I would say that I know your deepest secrets—for God is united to you, to your soul, and you will never be able to escape His omnipresent Sight. Why try to turn your back on Him and lead your life without Him?

THE HOLY POPE SPEAKS: Saint John Paul II

I say unto you, I say unto you verily, God loves you and He is ready today to give you His Infinite Mercy when you introduce yourself to Him under my Divine Wing.

Say Yes to me now: "Yes, Saint John Paul II, my Friend and my Divine Benefactor, I accept that my soul be presented to God Almighty, and through the Gift of Holiness that was given to you, dear Saint John Paul II, intercede for my soul so that I also may become one day a Saint among the Saints in Paradise, singing hymns of praise and adoration to the Holy Trinity, in the Glory of the Heavenly Father. Amen. So be it."

Alleluia! Alleluia! Alleluia! Blessed is he who stands today before God, for today, God the Father is Merciful to him, by virtue of my Holiness ordained by God.

THE HOLY POPE SPEAKS Saint John Paul II

My beloved children, I am pleased to speak to you today about your soul. Your soul, seen from here above, is beautiful, glorious, and luminous as you are reading these Lines. What a great vision for us to behold!

However, when your soul is subject to the negativity that is too often life on earth, your soul becomes obscured, deformed, and sullied. How sorrowful for us in Heaven! For the state of your soul is what we observe about you and the salvation of your soul is our goal.

Take care of your soul as if it were the apple of your eyes! Do not ruin it with unhealthy and addictive activities; do not be fooled by individuals or groups proclaiming falsehoods with regard to the so-called benefits of a marginal and nonreligious life; do nothing that is negligent or abusive with respect to your physical body, for the soul always suffers the consequences.

On the contrary, be moderate in all behaviors addressing the maintenance of the human body, seek Spirituality and the significance of God in all aspects of your life, and stay away from individuals or groups who have allegedly found a sense of life that excludes God. Above all, pray, pray, pray, directly to God the Father, and indirectly through all the messengers of God who carry your requests toward God.

THE HOLY POPE SPEAKS: Saint John Paul II

For God, Supreme Sovereign Who governs the world, knows the details of your soul at every moment of the day or night, and consequently decides your destiny in matters regarding the following moment of the day or night.

Alleluia! Alleluia! Alleluia! Blessed is he who cares for his soul, for God Himself will take care of him.

Amen. Alleluia!

THE HOLY POPE SPEAKS: Saint John Paul II

My children,

I speak to you with a Divine Faith entirely and eternally devoted to the cause of the salvation of your soul. My human faith has been transformed into Divine Faith by virtue of the Grace of God, who was Merciful on my own soul after the passage that is death. My Divine Faith means that my intentions and desires have a Cosmic Force and a miraculous effectiveness before God that you cannot understand because of the limitations of the human intellect.

My Divine Faith is a Gift from God that allows me to actualize my goals in Heaven, utilizing all the resources available here from whence I speak to you— the Holy Spirit, the Angels of God and their hierarchy, other Saints in Paradise, the Logos of the universe, the pure Souls, and other instruments of the Cosmic Law subject to God that you do not know.

My Divine Faith, consequently, can accomplish anything according to the intentions and requests that I submit personally to God the Father, and according to the final and ultimate Decision of God the Father Almighty, which becomes written in His Great Plan of Salvation for humanity.

THE HOLY POPE SPEAKS: Saint John Paul II

My Divine Faith is now focusing on you, dear reader, dear child, and I promise you to keep your little soul, which is being embellished day by day, very close to me, Saint John Paul II, and very close to God, our Creator of all.

Alleluia! Alleluia! Alleluia! Blessed is he who becomes the object of my Divine Faith, for God the Father Almighty shall be clement unto him.

Amen. Alleluia!

THE HOLY POPE SPEAKS — Saint John Paul II

My children, today, I wish to speak to you about Divine Faith. Divine Faith is unique among the Gifts from Heaven. Divine Faith defines my own and unique Will to pray on your behalf before God, in my capacity as a Saint in Paradise, and according to the virtues and attributes I have accumulated during my life.

All God's children are equal in His Eyes. However, our Divine Nature (among the Saints in Paradise) is unique and individualized as well, owing to our unique and individualized experiences on earth and the specificity of our missions on earth as in Heaven.

My Divine Faith, therefore, defines my own Will to influence the Will of the Father on your behalf, owing to my unique position before God. Indeed, all of the Saints in Paradise hold their unique and individualized Divine Faith that God the Father honors and glorifies. Every Saint in Paradise holds a unique position before God and our prayers are added and contribute to what is called the Divine Providence toward you.

THE HOLY POPE SPEAKS: Saint John Paul II

We, the inhabitants of Paradise, are working unceasingly on your behalf, in order to support you, guide you, and protect you. In particular, our prayers offered to God the Father, expressed according to our individual and Divine Faith, modify your life at levels much more numerous and complex than you can imagine.

Alleluia! Alleluia! Alleluia! Blessed is he who prays to the Saints in Paradise, for the Divine Faith animating us will animate you, as well.

Amen. So be it.

J✝✝✝✝✝ PII

THE HOLY POPE SPEAKS — Saint John Paul II

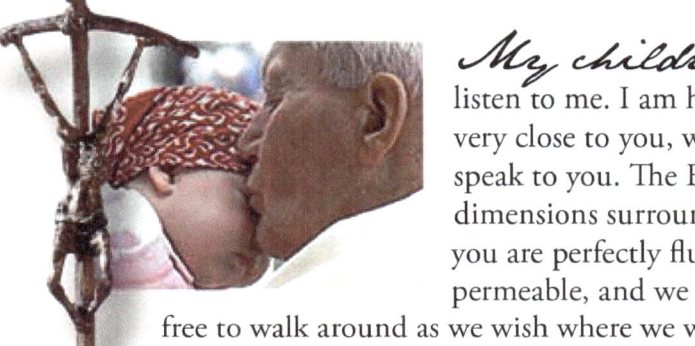

My children, listen to me. I am here, very close to you, when I speak to you. The Etheric dimensions surrounding you are perfectly fluid and permeable, and we are free to walk around as we wish where we want on earth.

In addition, I am capable of influencing your thinking at any moment and about anything. I can inform you instantly of an effective solution regarding a problem assailing you. Here is the origin of your Eureka moments, when the light suddenly illuminates a complex situation in your life!

In a nutshell: I love you and I wish to assist you in every step of your life and at all levels. I will teach you shortly the preferred and effective methods to interact with us, the Saints in Paradise.

Alleluia! Alleluia! Alleluia!
Blessed is he who seeks
the assistance of the Saints in Paradise,
for God the Father Almighty
in this is pleased.

Amen. So be it.

THE HOLY POPE SPEAKS — Saint John Paul II

My children, listen to the Words of the Master Jesus through His messengers on earth. The messengers of Christ Jesus are many among you: the members of the clergy, the Apostles of the Bible, the servants of God who have received private revelations in the course of history.

Be assured that Marie-Josée T. is a messenger of God. Marie-Josée is the essence of Saint Paul on earth. Her gift of clairvoyance and clairaudience allows her to hear me and see me with the eyes of the heart. Marie-Josée receives dictations and messages from the inhabitants of Paradise as well as from Christ every day.

Shortly, it will be obvious to you that this servant of God, blessed by God and intimate with Christ, is truly a vessel chosen by God Himself in order to share with you the Good News of His Kingdom during these sorrowful times in the history of humanity. For the events that lie ahead require a special preparation which I undertake to communicate to you here.

Alleluia! Alleluia! Alleluia! Blessed be Marie-Josée, for she obeys the commandments of God and works relentlessly for humanity, in her apostolic capacity as messenger of Christ and servant of God.

Amen. So be it.

My children, listen to me. I am here, very close to you, when I speak to you. The etheric dimensions surrounding you are perfectly fluid and permeable, and we are free to walk around as we wish where we want on earth.

Alleluia! Alleluia! Alleluia! Blessed is he who seeks the assistance of the Saints in Paradise, for God the Father Almighty in this is pleased. Amen. So be it.
~ Saint John Paul II

THE HOLY POPE SPEAKS — Saint John Paul II

My beloved children, I take you in my arms! Today, I speak to you about faith.

Faith in God, my children, is all you need to go through all the stages of your life, including the tragic events that lie ahead.

Have a firm and unshakable faith in the One Who created you, Who loved you even before creating you, in fact, and still loves you now, and always, for ever and ever.

I say unto you, I say unto you verily, your destiny on earth as in Heaven is based solely on your faith in Him, God the Father Almighty, our Creator of all, through His Only and Beloved Son, our Lord Jesus Christ, and our Divine Mother, the Most Blessed Virgin Mary.

Alleluia! Alleluia! Alleluia! Blessed is he who has faith in God, for God will give him Paradise.

Amen. So be it.

THE HOLY POPE SPEAKS: Saint John Paul II

My children,
I will be with you until the end of time—and beyond. For the Father has decided so. He, the Absolute Master of the universe known and unknown to men, has sanctified my soul. I am infinitely grateful to God the Father Almighty for such Grace and such Mercy on us all.

Today, my children of peace, I wish to tell you a secret. My soul has been sanctified by God—it is true—and it has also been ennobled by Christ Jesus Himself. As a result, from this Unique Cosmic Miracle, He has allowed me to enter within His Christic Light. Consequently, my soul is bathed in His Light that illuminates the world.

This means for you that when you pray directly to Christ, the Only Son of God, my soul thereby comes running to you in order to assist you and contribute to the awakening of your Consciousness in Christ.

You will surely recall that I implemented the Luminous Mysteries of the Rosary during my Papacy. The Holy Spirit acted within me at the time so as to inspire this revelation

The Holy Pope Speaks: Saint John Paul II

derived from Christ and honoring Christ. The Light of Christ had begun to burn inside my soul when I was human and Pope, and It extended to encompass all my soul with His Divine Majesty after the passage that is death—in 2005.

I am infinitely grateful and exalted to live in the Beatitude and the Glory of the Light of Christ that illuminates the world; and I hasten and work very hard at this point in the history of humanity in order to activate and multiply the Light of Christ all over the earth.

For shortly, after the events that are approaching have passed, the earth will be flooded with and embellished by the Grace and the Glory of the Light of Christ in all the Splendor that is Jesus the Christ our Savior and our God.

Alleluia! Alleluia! Alleluia! Blessed are those invited to live in the Light of Christ, for shortly everything will be nothing but Light of Christ.

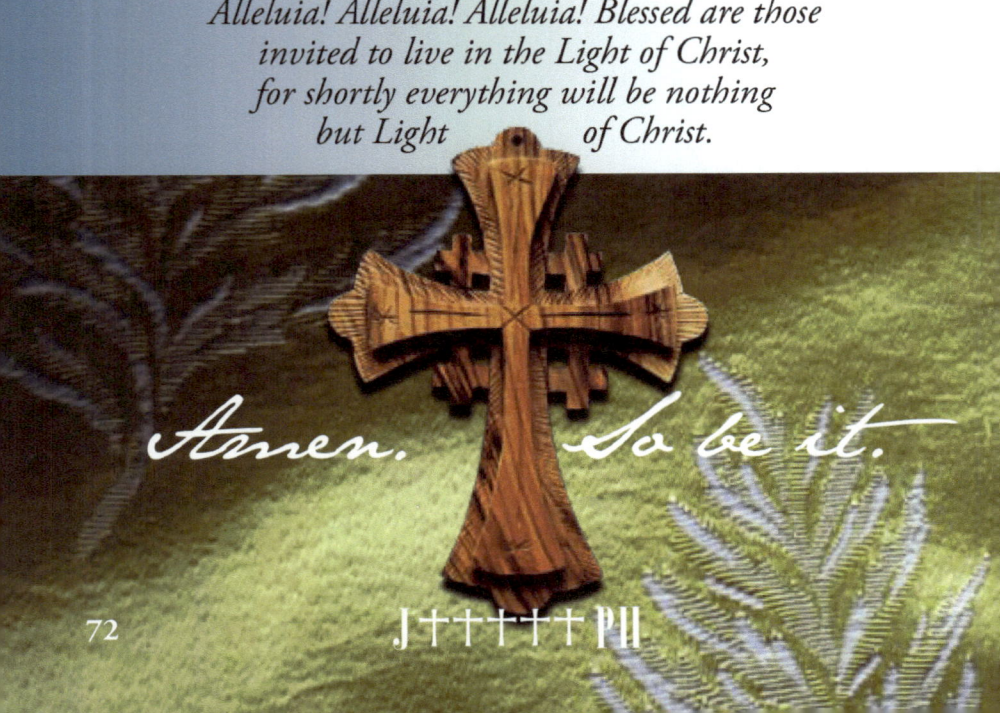

Amen.   So be it.

THE HOLY POPE SPEAKS: Saint John Paul II

My children,
I illuminate you with the Light of Christ, and my Gift for humanity, which began during my life on earth, is to illuminate you with the Light of Christ in the same way and just as equally.

Come, my children, come into the Light! The Light of Christ beams in your heart with Splendor and Glory unsurpassed in the entire universe! Come and live in Christ, the Light of the world, our Savior and our God! Amen. Alleluia!

Alleluia! Alleluia! Alleluia! Blessed is he who walks in the Light of Christ, for God the Father Almighty also illuminates him with the Graces of Heaven.

Amen. So be it.

THE HOLY POPE SPEAKS: Saint John Paul II

My children, remain in the Light and the Light will guide you to the Kingdom of Heaven! Follow my example.

When I lived on earth, as early as my childhood, I was intrigued by the concept of Light, of peace, of an ideal solution brought about for any problem, and above all, of social harmony and coexistence among nations. Where are these concepts assembled in a totality, at once transcendent, powerful, and loving? Jesus Christ is the answer to everything, for He is Everything, He is the very Foundation at the basis of Life on earth.

I say unto you, I say unto you verily, Christ Jesus, my Lord and my God, represents everything you need in order to return to God, for He is truly the Way, the Truth, and the Life.

Alleluia! Alleluia! Alleluia! Blessed is he that comes in the Name of the Lord, for God the Father Almighty will open the Gates of Paradise to him.

Amen. Alleluia!

THE HOLY POPE SPEAKS Saint John Paul II

My children, be strong and righteous in all the decisions of your life. Adopt the attitude of a child of God who is courageous, generous, charitable, honest and compassionate toward your fellowman.

Observe and apply all the Teachings of Christ the Savior. Love and forgive! Pray and pray again! Go to church regularly and submit yourself to confession often! Receive the Body of Christ through the Sacrament of the Eucharist often! Read the Bible, the religious books written by the Saints in history and the story of their lives, and the teaching materials provided by the Church!

And particularly, particularly, read the books dictated by other Saints in Paradise to the essence of Saint Paul on earth, Marie-Josée T. For these books are blessed by God Himself and are written within His Great Plan of Salvation for humanity.

For the end times are near, the minutes go by fast, and the state of your soul is what you need to be preoccupied with from this moment and henceforth.

Alleluia! Alleluia! Alleluia! Blessed is he who imitates Christ Jesus now, for now is the time chosen by God to assess the state of this soul.

Amen. So be it.

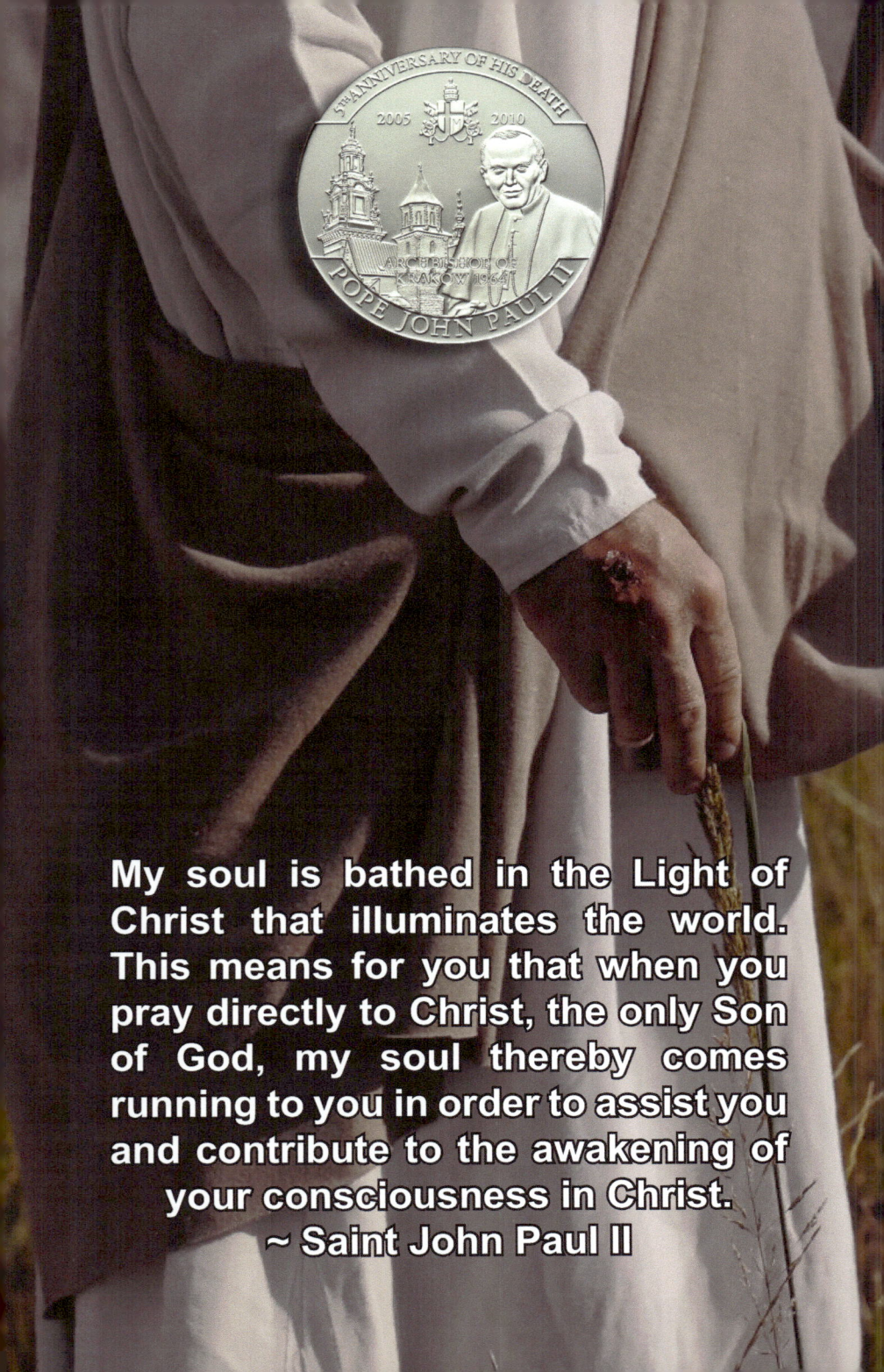

My soul is bathed in the Light of Christ that illuminates the world. This means for you that when you pray directly to Christ, the only Son of God, my soul thereby comes running to you in order to assist you and contribute to the awakening of your consciousness in Christ.
~ Saint John Paul II

THE HOLY POPE SPEAKS — Saint John Paul II

My children, be humble in your relationships with others. Never let vanity and the attraction for personal gain influence your judgment and your mind. Remember that at every moment of your life, God is observing you and God is testing you, for He wishes to behold your soul white as snow and purified. God loves you so much!

I bless you in the Name of the Father, and of the Son, and of the Holy Spirit.

Alleluia! Alleluia! Alleluia!
Blessed are the meek at heart,
for God the Father Almighty therein rejoices.

Amen. Alleluia!

THE HOLY POPE SPEAKS — Saint John Paul II

My children,
I am honored to be a servant of God, and also to be at the service of the salvation of your soul. When I was Pope, I was so dedicated and filled with wonder by the mission God had given me on earth!

Now, today, your soul is in my hands, and I promise you today to accomplish to perfection what God has asked me to do concerning your soul: to bring it to His Kingdom, the House of God awaiting you, which is incomplete without your precious presence.

For you, dear reader, are a beloved child of God, and God desires at the highest degree to demonstrate His Intimate Presence and His Love for you through my Holy and Divine intervention.

Alleluia! Alleluia! Alleluia!
Blessed are those invited
to the Kingdom of God,
for God Himself
has invited them.

Amen. So be it.

THE HOLY POPE SPEAKS — Saint John Paul II

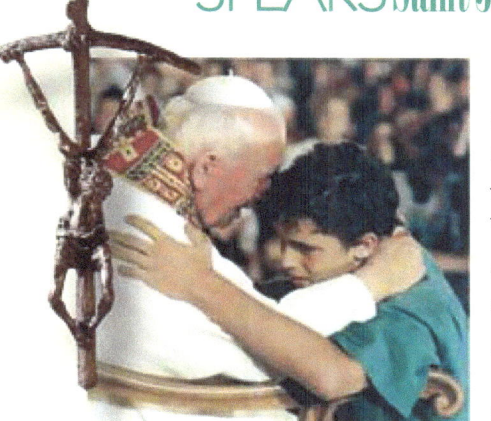

My children, my friends, I want to speak today about the virtue of compassion. When I was Pope on earth, the virtue of compassion had deepened within me.

I observed so many contradictions in the world of men, such suffering due to the immoralities of society. I witnessed so much abuse, such negligence, so many violations of human dignity in what concerns the basic needs of life on earth—for example, the need to feed oneself and one's family, for shelter, for clothing, for the fulfillment of one's potential. I observed so much suffering in the human heart that my own heart became filled with compassion and love for humanity in the grip of despair.

This compassion within me had become one of the deep motivations for my visits around the world and my desire to establish personal contacts with ailing hearts.

The virtue of compassion is a Grace from God that is dear to Him. Compassion is of Divine Origin for it is rooted in God Who is Compassion itself. God is Compassion, God is Love, God is Mercy before human suffering.

Do not fall into despair and despondency when suffering overwhelms you. On the contrary, turn to God immediately, for that is what He expects from you—and pray. God is The

THE HOLY POPE SPEAKS — Saint John Paul II

One Who has allowed this temporary suffering in your life in order to increase your faith and the fervor of your prayers, and that is when God takes great pleasure in comforting you and consoling you. God is at the Source of everything in your life, as much in the suffering as the remedy for this same suffering, and this remedy will appear more or less quickly depending on your level of surrender to His Will. Do you see?

Love God in everything that He commands with regard to your life and God will let you see His Compassion while teaching you the virtue of compassion for your fellowmen.

Alleluia! Alleluia! Alleluia!
Blessed are the hearts of compassion,
for God Himself lives therein.

J †††††† PII

THE HOLY POPE SPEAKS — Saint John Paul II

My children, always remain in the Light of Christ! I have already said so and I repeat it today and every day of your life! Christ is the Way, the Truth, and the Life! He alone is our Savior! Be not afraid! He alone brings us to Eternal Life! He alone is the Light of the world! Such Grace is to know Christ and to come closer to Him every day.

When I was Pope, my enchantment for Christ increased every day, as a result of my love for Him and my faith in Him, but above all because His Glorious Presence revealed itself more and more within me. I could feel His physical Presence at my right, and I could hear His Words of teaching, of instruction and of consolation inside my heart. Christ Jesus speaks to you every day, despite the fact that you may not be listening to Him.

Be not afraid!
Open wide the doors
to Christ Jesus!
And He will
reveal Himself to you!

Amen. Alleluia!

30 — THE HOLY POPE SPEAKS — Saint John Paul II

My children,
I am so happy to be able to speak to you today! My communication with the world has always been fundamental in my life.

When I became Pope, my communication with the Catholic and non-Catholic world intensified and evolved on several levels in order to change attitudes and ways of thinking, as well as to open the hearts and expand the faith in God by everyone.

I am infinitely grateful to God the Father Almighty for giving me the Voice once again, through Marie-Josée T., the essence of Saint Paul on earth. Be assured that my Voice is communicated to you in a sacred, integral, and authentic way, without alteration on her part. Marie-Josée is a vessel of the Grace of God and a messenger for the whole Heaven. Several Saints in Paradise Who are part of her Celestial Court speak to her every day, in addition to Christ Jesus, the Virgin Mary, and her Father Saint Paul, who also speaks to her every day.

Marie-Josée has for her mission to communicate the Voices from Heaven to you, dear inhabitant of the earth, thanks to the Divine Mercy won by the five crosses of the Legion of Saint Paul, and granted by the Will of God the Father Almighty Who loves you, and Who decides everything taking place on earth.

THE HOLY POPE SPEAKS: Saint John Paul II

Rest well assured, thus, I repeat it unto you, that the Sacred Words you are reading, and the Holy and Compassionate Voice you are hearing through these Lines, are truly from me, Saint John Paul II, servant of God and sanctified by God, through the intervention of the essence of Saint Paul on earth, Marie-Josée T., blessed by God and carried by God.

Alleluia! Alleluia! Alleluia!
Blessed are those invited to the Mercy
won by the five crosses of the Legion of Saint Paul.

Amen. So be it!

God is at the source of everything in your life, as much in the suffering as the remedy for this same suffering, and this remedy will appear more or less quickly depending on your level of surrender to His Will. Do you see?
~ Saint John Paul II

THE HOLY POPE SPEAKS — Saint John Paul II

My children,
I am in Heaven and from here I can accomplish a thousand times more than on earth. My Holy and Divine Powers have multiplied after the passage that is death—in 2005—by the Great and Benevolent Grace of God, the Father Almighty.

The Virgin Mary, my Divine Mother, our Mother to all (even here in Paradise), protected me during my life on earth, and She and I have spiritually united in Paradise. The Most Holy, Most Glorious Virgin Mary, is everywhere on earth as in Heaven, and Her mission also intensifies every day, by Decision of the Father, because of the events that lie ahead.

Pray very often to the Most Blessed Mary ever-Virgin, for She hears every prayer made to Her, for Her Love and Her Powers are unique and ineffable among the Treasures in Paradise.

Alleluia! Alleluia! Alleluia! Blessed be the Virgin Mary, the Mother of Christ, present in us and everywhere, on earth as in Heaven!

Amen. So be it.

THE HOLY POPE SPEAKS — Saint John Paul II

My children, I am pleased that this life given to you by God will be taken by God when you return to His House, the Kingdom of Heaven.

Imagine life without God! Impossible! God is Everything; the Divine Trinity is the Foundation of everything, and life on earth—all life that multiplies in the human, animal, plant and mineral worlds—is fundamentally of Christic Matter, of Energy emanating from Jesus Christ, and filled with His Glorious Light. Look at a flower and know that this flower holds Christ in it.

*Jesus Christ, our Lord and our God,
truly is the Way, the Truth, and the Life!*

Amen. Alleluia!

THE HOLY POPE SPEAKS — Saint John Paul II

My children,
I am honored to be part of your life, for your soul is so precious to me and to the Father Almighty.

God loves all His children equally, perfectly, completely and eternally. Who else can give you everything you need to live, including the very Source of the Fire that is Life? God is at the origin of Life, of all the Creation, for He is the Divine Fire of the Central Sun, the Cradle of the universe.

God conferred on His Only Son the Sovereignty over Life animating all His creatures. The Christic Energy is the Foundation of Life itself, this current of Fire uniting us to God and bringing us back to God through the universal cycle that God Himself has imposed.

Alleluia! Alleluia! Alleluia!
Blessed is he who respects and honors every life,
for Jesus the Christ Himself
receives this respect and honor.

Amen. Alleluia!

THE HOLY POPE SPEAKS — Saint John Paul II

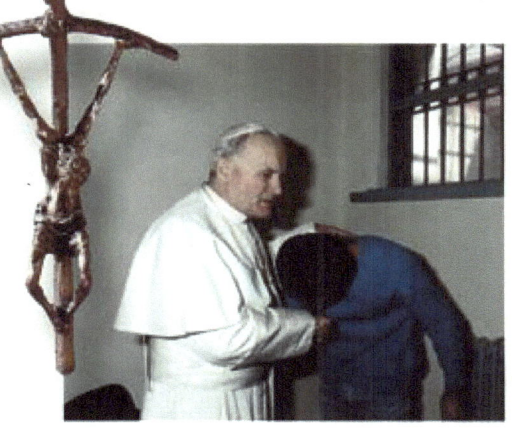

My children, remain pure and white as snow! For God the Father Almighty sees everything, hears everything, and knows everything concerning everyone inhabiting the earth. The Father loves you and wishes to hold you in His Almighty Arms upon your return to Paradise, in His House, the Kingdom of Heaven.

Be fair and responsible vis-à-vis your fellowman, be loving and kind, be flexible and cooperative, be attentive and respectful, remain in truth and righteousness always. For God the Father will hold you accountable concerning every moment of your life that took place outside the Holy Light of Christ on Judgment Day after the passage that is death.

*Alleluia! Alleluia! Alleluia!
Blessed is he who fears the Judgment of God
for God shall be Merciful unto him.*

Amen, Alleluia!

35

THE HOLY POPE SPEAKS — Saint John Paul II

My children, be not afraid! I repeat it again today, as I have repeated it thousands of times and in several languages when I was Pope: be not afraid!

Fear is a ploy generated by the devil in order to make you waste time, to turn you away from God, and to make you fall, due to the resulting false anxiety! Be not afraid, for God the Father loves you. The Holy Trinity dwells in your heart and you are therefore equipped with everything you need to combat any adversity!

Fear is empty of meaning and reality. It is a weakness in your Etheric body, it is a portal of entry for the green snake that is the enemy, wishing to infiltrate and infect your life with negativity.

Be not afraid and open wide the doors to Christ Jesus, the Only and Universal Source of Peace! Amen. Alleluia!

THE HOLY POPE SPEAKS: Saint John Paul II

Say often: "O God, come to my aid! O Lord, make haste to help me! Amen!" And by means of this very powerful prayer, fear dissipates and Christ Jesus pours in Light and Peace unto you. Be not afraid and pray!

*Alleluia! Alleluia! Alleluia!
Blessed is he who prays always,
for Christ is always with him.*

J††††††PII

AFTERWORD

Saint John Paul II stood by your side as you were reading this book. Did you feel his presence?

He said, "Saint John Paul II, the Pope you have known and loved and in whom you have put all your trust and all your hope, will never abandon you. I promise you. I am Saint John Paul II, and I love you."

What a beautiful and powerful message! Be not afraid!

Saint John Paul II, I love you!

Marie-Josée

ABOUT THE AUTHOR

Marie-Josée Thibault's life is in no way similar to yours. When she wakes, the saints of Heaven visit her, talk to her, teach her, and pray intensely with her. When such mystical sessions draw to a close, she greets with great respect and deep reverence the Masters of the Heavenly Court. This servant of the Lord spends the rest of the day in the company of her guardian angel, who continues her spiritual education and ceaselessly protects her from the perils of this fallen world.

Bestowed by the Heavenly Father, her gifts of clairvoyance and clairaudience allow her to remain in continuous contact with the supernatural dimension juxtaposed with ours, where the soul is born of the Spirit through Jesus and Mary. She prays that, one day soon, the entire human race will give glory to the Father, the Son, and the Holy Spirit.

ALSO BY THE AUTHOR

- Saint Padre Pio Speaks: Book 1
- Abba, Your Father, Speaks: Book I
- Abba, Your Father, Speaks: Book II
- Angel Gabriel Speaks: Book 1
- Saint Beethoven Speaks: Book 1
- Dear Humanity: Book 1
- Dear Humanity: Book 2
- Saint Barnabas Speaks: Book 1
- Saint Bernadette Speaks Book 1
- Saint Therese of Lisieux Speaks: Book 1
- Saint Joan of Arc Speaks: Book 1
- Saint Martin de Porres Speaks - Book 1

Pray, my children, pray again!

~ Saint John Paul II

Saint John Paul II
Karol Wojtyla
(1920-2005)

FREE DOWNLOAD

Get your free copy of :
"Saint Padre Pio Speaks: Book 1" when you sign up to the author's VIP mailing list! Get started here:

www.abbamyfatheriloveyou.com